PLANET UNDER PRESSURE
POLLUTION

Clive Gifford

Heinemann Library
Chicago, Illinois

S

J
363.73
GIF

Editorial: Sarah Shannon
and Louise Galpine
Design: Lucy Owen and Bridge
Creative Services Ltd
Picture Research: Natalie Gray
and Sally Cole
Production: Chloe Bloom

Printed and bound in China by South
China Printing Company

10 09 08 07 06
10 9 8 7 6 5 4 3 2 1

Library of Congress Cataloging-in-Publication Data

Gifford, Clive.
  Pollution / Clive Gifford.
    p. cm. -- (Planet under pressure)
  Includes bibliographical references and
index.
  ISBN 1-4034-7742-6 (library binding-hardcover : alk. paper)
  1. Pollution--Juvenile literature. I. Title. II.
Series.
  TD176.G54 2006
  363.73--dc22

2005017064

Acknowledgments
The publishers would like to thank the
following for permission to reproduce
copyright material: Alamy pp. **10–11**
(Bryan & Cherry Alexander); Corbis pp.
14–15; Corbis pp. **20–21** (W. Geiersperger),
24–25 (Nathan Benn), **28–29** (Angelo
Harnak), **32** (Ashley Cooper), **38** (Keren
Su); **12–13** (Steve Marcus / Las Vegas / Sun
/ Reuters); Corbis/Bettmann pp. **16–17;**
Corbis/Sygma pp. **36** (Les Stone);
DEBKUSHAL/UNEP/Still Pictures pp. **3–4,**
6–7; Digital Vision/Harcourt Education Ltd
pp. **24–25;** Empics/EPA pp. **16–17, 36–37;**
Environmental Images pp. **36** (Herbert
Girardet); Panos pp. **8–9** (Mark Henley),
12–13 (Chris Stowers), **26–27** (Caroline
Penn), **32–33** (Karen Robinson); Panos/
Visum pp. **22–23** (Ludwig Gerd); Science
Photo Library pp. **28–29** (Simon Fraser);
Science Photo Library/NOAA pp. **18–19;**
Still Pictures pp. **10–11** (Al Grillo), **30--31**
(Mark Edwards), **34–35** (Hartmut
Schwarzbach), **40–41** (Ray Pfortner).

Cover photograph of pipe with pollution
reproduced with kind permission of Getty
and of city with heavy pollution from pipes
with kind permission of Still Pictures.

Every effort has been made to contact
copyright holders of any material
reproduced in this book. Any omissions
will be rectified in subsequent printings if
notice is given to the publishers.

The paper used to print this book comes
from sustainable resources.

Dedicated to the memory of Lucy Owen

Contents

Any words appearing in the text in bold,
like this, are explained in the Glossary.

Pollution Issues Around the World

NORTH
AMERICA

Read page 31 to find
out how the dumping
of **toxic** chemicals
created a major
environmental hazard
at Love Canal in the
United States.

Learn on page 25 how
pollution has caused a giant
dead zone in the waters of
part of the Gulf of Mexico.

ATLANTIC
OCEAN

Pollution prevents millions of people
from having access to clean, safe
water supplies. Read on page 8
about how polluted water helped
spread the disease of **cholera**
throughout Peru in the early 1990s.

SOUTH
AMERICA

PACIFIC
OCEAN

N

Severe air pollution can kill. Read on page 16 about how **smog** in London killed more than 12,000 people.

Pollution is a global problem. Pollution generated in one part of the world affects others. Read on page 11 about the pollution problems faced by the Inuit peoples of the Arctic Circle.

Dumping of radioactive waste into Lake Karachai has made it one of the most polluted locations on Earth. Find out more on page 23.

Learn about the attempts to clean up the heavily polluted Lake Taihu in China on page 38.

The Pacific island nation of Tuvalu faces devastation as a result of rising sea levels caused by global warming. Learn more on page 21.

EUROPE

ASIA

AFRICA

INDIAN OCEAN

AUSTRALIA

A Global Problem

Pollution occurs all over the planet on land, in water, and at both low and high **altitudes** in Earth's **atmosphere**. Pollution is the introduction of a substance or energy at levels that cause harm to living things or the **environment**. Scientists think of pollution mainly in terms of the introduction of pollutants by human activity. Pollution can vary in scale from a single car's exhaust **emissions** to a giant factory pumping thousands of gallons of chemical waste water into rivers.

Wrong place, wrong amount

A pollutant may occur harmlessly in nature, but when it is released into a certain location, or at too high a concentration, it has harmful effects. For instance, ozone performs a useful role high in the atmosphere, but if it is released at ground level, ozone can be a dangerous pollutant.

Sometimes the amount, concentration, or location of a substance causes pollution. For example, carbon dioxide (CO_2) occurs in nature and is part of the collection of gases that make up our atmosphere. People, animals, and plants generate it naturally as a byproduct of **respiration**. However, over the last 200 years, the burning of **fossil fuels** has sent millions of tons of extra carbon dioxide into the atmosphere. This additional carbon dioxide has resulted in the **enhanced greenhouse effect**, which is a major part of **global warming** (see page 20).

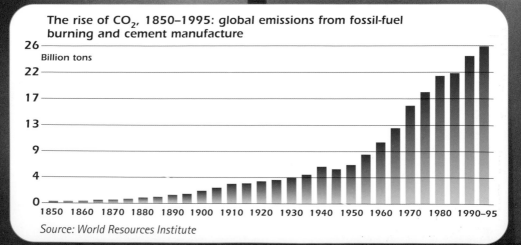

The rise of CO_2, 1850–1995: global emissions from fossil-fuel burning and cement manufacture

Billion tons

26
22
17
13
9
4
0

1850 1860 1870 1880 1890 1900 1910 1920 1930 1940 1950 1960 1970 1980 1990–95

Source: World Resources Institute

Carrying chemicals

Chemicals enter people's bodies from the air they breathe, the water they drink, and the food they eat. In 2005, a study by the U.S. Centers for Disease Control and Prevention found that most of the 2,400 Americans tested were carrying dozens of pesticides and toxic compounds in their bodies. Many of these chemicals are not easily broken down and remain in people's bodies. The study, the largest of its kind ever undertaken, found more than 100 different toxic compounds carried in the test subjects.

Source: CDC, 2005

When did pollution start?

Pollution is not new. Ever since humans started consuming the planet's **resources**, there has been some pollution. In the past, the impact on the planet was minimal. Smoke from fires, human **sewage** in water, and other pollutants were gradually broken down or absorbed by the environment. But as the world population grew and people started to settle together in large towns and cities, local pollution became a problem.

COAL

One of the earliest recorded instances of **urban** air pollution was in the 12th century. People in London began to burn coal instead of wood. This caused so much choking smoke and smog that the King of England, Edward I, threatened coal burners with execution. Later, in 1880, London again suffered severe air pollution from coal burning, resulting in more than 2,000 deaths.

WATER-BORNE PROBLEMS

Many of the world's early urban areas had little or no sewage treatment or waste disposal systems. Waste and sewage flowing into rivers polluted the water, making it undrinkable and providing ideal conditions for deadly diseases. **Cholera** thrives in sewage-polluted water: it is spread by **ingesting** water, food, or any other material containing bacteria from the human waste of a cholera victim. Polluted water caused a cholera **epidemic** that swept through South America in 1991 and killed 2,720 people in Peru, and another 4,000 in neighboring countries.

Top ten most polluted cities, 2000

1. Lanzhou, China
2. Guangzhou, China
3. Shanghai, China
4. Xian, China
5. Shenyang, China
6. Mumbai, India
7. Kolkata, India
8. Mexico City, Mexico
9. Seoul, South Korea
10. New Delhi, India

Source: World Health Organization

INDUSTRY AND POPULATION GROWTH

Beginning with the industrial revolution in the mid-18th century, more and more goods have been made in large factories and consumed by a rapidly growing population. In the 20th century, the world's population quadrupled to more than six billion people. Many of these people, especially in the wealthier, more developed nations, consume more goods and create more waste and pollution than ever before. With the invention of cars, airplanes, and many electrical items, world consumption of energy has increased more than ten times during the same period. Fossil fuels are the main energy sources we use to produce electricity and drive motor vehicles. Burning fossil fuels releases large amounts of pollutants into the atmosphere.

Year	World population	World popultion living in urban areas	
1000	300,000,000	2%	
1700	700,000,000	2%	
1800	1,000,000,000	3%	
1900	1,700,000,000	15%	
1950	2,500,000,000	30%	
1970	3,700,000,000	36%	
1990	5,300,000,000	43%	
2000	6,100,000,000	47%	
2010	6,800,000,000	51%	(estimated)
2030	8,100,000,000	61%	(estimated)

Source: United Nations Population Division

A global issue

For many years, pollution was considered a local problem. But a series of major environmental accidents began to change people's thinking. Major oil spills from tankers, such as the *Torrey Canyon* and *Exxon Valdez,* which devastated coastal wildlife and communities, were worldwide news. So were the fears of radiation pollution (see page 23) from accidents and leaks at nuclear power plants or during the transportation of radioactive waste.

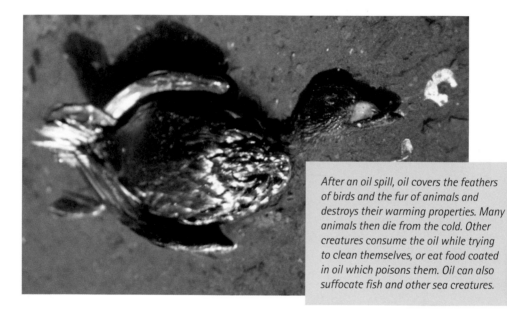

After an oil spill, oil covers the feathers of birds and the fur of animals and destroys their warming properties. Many animals then die from the cold. Other creatures consume the oil while trying to clean themselves, or eat food coated in oil which poisons them. Oil can also suffocate fish and other sea creatures.

As the 20th century progressed, scientists and environmentalists realized that pollution occurred on a global scale. Public awareness was raised by reports of how certain toxic chemicals, such as **insecticides**, were used in one area but transported through water or air over long distances. Scientists discovered, for instance, that in remote parts of Greenland, 1,000 miles (1,600 kilometers) from the nearest major road, lead particles emitted by car exhausts had been trapped in the ice in air bubbles.

During the late 1970s and the 1980s, three major global pollution issues emerged: the hole in the **ozone layer** (see page 18), **acid rain** (page 18), and global warming (page 20). All three of these environmental problems cross national boundaries and affect entire regions, continents, or even the entire planet.

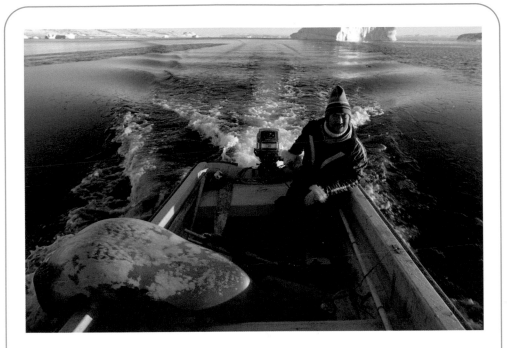

Arctic Circle polluted by Asia, America, and Africa

Pollutants from as far away as Mexico and China threaten the traditional
food sources of the native Inuit peoples living inside the Arctic Circle.
Harmful agricultural pesticides have been carried by wind across oceans and
continents to the frozen Arctic, which scientists believe acts as a sponge for
a wide range of pollutants. Some of these pollutants find their way into the
food chain where they are carried in animal fats. The traditional Inuit diet
is based heavily on animal fats from fish and sea mammals, such as seals.
A report by the Canadian Polar Commission warns that concentrations of
these substances could reach dangerous levels in the next few decades.

Pollution today

In recent times, most countries have passed laws or started initiatives to
combat rising levels of pollution. As the following chapters show, there
are many things people, governments, and industries can do to help
prevent and reduce pollution. But the problem of pollution is still a
growing one. It affects millions of people's health and the land or
water they rely on to survive.

Air Pollution

The atmosphere is the mixture of gases that surround a body in space. Other planets have an atmosphere but, so far, Earth is the only planet known to possess an atmosphere capable of supporting life. Its gases are essential for the functioning of almost all living things. The atmosphere also plays a key role in the water cycle (see page 22), in which wind and air currents transport rain around the globe. The atmosphere also shields the planet's surface from certain harmful rays from the Sun while trapping enough heat to warm the planet for life to flourish.

Carbon dioxide 0.03%

Argon, Helium
Neon
0.07%

*Composition of
Earth's atmosphere*

Oxygen
21%

Nitrogen
78%

Emissions of gases into the air are not caused solely by human activity. Sulphur dioxide (SO_2) and nitrogen oxides (NO_x) both can occur in the atmosphere as a result of volcanic activity and the decay of dead animals and plants. The world's 1.3 billion cattle generate as much as 20 percent of the total **methane** emitted into the atmosphere. It is only in the past 250 years, since the world has **industrialized,** the world population boomed, and large areas of forest have been cleared, that air pollution emissions have risen to their current threatening levels.

The most polluted city in the United States

In 2004, a report by the American Lung Association ranked Los Angeles as the United States city with the worst air pollution. The city ranked worst in both smog levels and particle pollution (the microscopic particles produced by wood burning, diesel exhaust, power plant emissions, and various other sources). According to the report, more than 25 percent of Americans live in areas with unhealthy particle pollution levels. Nearly 50 percent live in areas where the smog levels are considered health-threatening. In 2005, a separate study found that people in the most polluted sections of Los Angeles were more likely to suffer from asthma, diabetes, and fatal heart disease. Researchers attribute the higher pollution levels to the city's size, number of automobiles, and location. Traffic congestion is common in the commuter-heavy city of 13 million people. Because the city sits in a valley surrounded by mountains, researchers believe this helps trap the pollution.

What are the main air pollutants?

There are many different air pollutants that cause harm at different locations in the atmosphere. Some of them are:

Carbon dioxide (CO_2) is produced in nature, but also by the burning of fossil fuels and wood. In addition to being the major **greenhouse gas,** rare, low-level clouds of carbon dioxide can kill. In 1986 a carbon dioxide cloud caused by volcanic activity around Lake Nyos in Cameroon (a republic in western Africa) killed 1,800 people.

Carbon monoxide (CO) is produced by the incomplete burning of wood and fossil fuels in transportation. It lowers the amount of oxygen that enters blood and mainly affects the heart and nervous system. Large quantities can cause death.

Chlorofluorocarbons (CFCs) are gases that are released mainly from air-conditioning systems, aerosols, and refrigeration. When emitted into the higher atmosphere they react with other substances to damage the ozone layer. At a lower level, they add to the enhanced greenhouse effect.

Lead (Pb) is present in some fuels, lead batteries, paints, and many other products. It can cause damage to the nervous system and digestive problems, and, in some cases, cancer. It especially affects children.

Nitrogen oxides (NO_x) help cause smog and acid rain. They are produced from burning fuels including gasoline, diesel, and coal. Nitrogen oxides, particularly nitrogen dioxide (NO_2), can cause major breathing problems, such as severe asthma.

Ozone (O_3) occurs naturally in the upper layers of the atmosphere, but ground-level ozone, produced by pollutants from vehicles and industries, is a dangerous part of smog causing eye irritation, breathing problems, and diseases.

Particulate matter (PM) consists of tiny solid particles in the air in the form of smoke, dust, and vapor that can remain suspended for long periods. PM10s are a type of particulate matter that can lodge in lungs, cause severe health problems, and even kill.

Sulphur dioxide (SO_2) is a gas produced mainly from burning coal in power plants and in industry. It is a major contributor to smog and acid rain. Sulphur dioxide can lead to lung diseases.

Major volcanic eruptions can send ash, soot, smoke, and chemicals high into the atmosphere. The 1991 eruption of Mount Pinatubo in the Philippines threw ash some 20 miles (32 kilometers) up into the atmosphere. Yet such natural emissions of gases are generally absorbed by Earth's atmosphere.

What is smog?

Smog is a mixture of air pollutants that can build up to extremely harmful concentrations, especially in crowded, urban areas. Smog often produces a haze that is difficult to see through. It can contain pollutants such as ammonia, nitrogen dioxide, carbon monoxide, and sulphur dioxide. However, the two most common and lethal pollutants are ground-level ozone and particulate matter (PM). Ground-level ozone is formed from complicated reactions in the air just above Earth's surface, involving nitrogen oxides and volatile organic compounds (VOCs).

Killer smog in Donora, Pennsylvania

In 1948, waste from a number of industries (including a zinc production plant and a steel mill) created a thick, heavily polluted smog over the valley of Donora, Pennsylvania. In five days more than 6,000 illnesses were reported and 20 people died.

In 1952, the United Kingdom experienced its worst reported air pollution disaster. A thick, heavily polluted fog shrouded London for four days. It was mainly caused by coal-burning in home fireplaces and in industry. It is now estimated that the smog caused 12,000 deaths.

WHY IS URBAN AIR POLLUTION SUCH A CONCERN?

Many of the key air pollutants that cause health problems are given off by motor vehicles and the burning of fossil fuels. When people and vehicles are crammed together in small areas, air pollution can rise to dangerous levels.

Clean air laws and cleaner fuels now required in many wealthier nations have reduced smog in their cities, but problems from ground-level ozone and particulate matter continue to exist. In the United States, particulate matter is estimated to cause 60,000 deaths per year.

Particulate matter is also partly responsible for millions of cases of breathing disorders, such as asthma, bronchitis, and pneumonia. The number of people suffering from asthma is rising; in the United States alone, more than six million children are asthma sufferers. Elsewhere in the world, especially in rapidly developing nations in Asia and Africa, the problems of air pollution are even more severe. China is home to half of the ten cities suffering from the worst air pollution in the world.

Mexico City

One of the world's most polluted cities, Mexico City is set in a basin almost completely surrounded by hills and mountains. This helps trap air pollution, which reacts chemically with strong sunlight to form ground-level ozone. The basin is home to an estimated twenty million people and more than four million motor vehicles. Levels of key pollutants like ozone and nitrogen dioxide are many times the maximum safe limits. According to the World Health Organization, some 6,400 people die every year and more than one million suffer from permanent breathing problems due to air pollution there.

The ozone layer

At ground level, ozone is a dangerous pollutant, but when it is high in the atmosphere it shields Earth's surface from the Sun's harmful **ultraviolet** rays. These rays can damage plant and ocean life, and cause skin cancers and other serious health problems. In 1985, British scientists discovered a hole (a very thinned area) approximately the size of the United States in the ozone layer above Antarctica. In addition, the entire global ozone layer was found to have thinned slightly.

The chief cause was believed to be the emission into the atmosphere of CFCs, chemicals that have only been produced since the 1930s. Chlorine is produced by the reaction of CFCs with ultraviolet rays from the Sun. One **atom** of chlorine can help to destroy 100,000 ozone molecules. CFCs break up slowly, and scientists estimate that even if no more were sent into the atmosphere, it would take many years for the ozone layer to recover.

This computer-generated image is a satellite map of the Antarctic region. The hole in the ozone layer is clearly shown as a dark blue area in the center.

Acid rain

Pollution can be transferred to the sea or land and across country's borders. One example of this is acid rain. Sulphur dioxide and nitrogen oxides, particularly from coal-burning industries, can mix with water vapor in the air. These pollutants then fall as acid rain. Acid rain **erodes** stone, kills trees, and destroys life in rivers and, especially, lakes. Winds and air currents can cause acid rain to fall long distances from where the pollutants were generated.

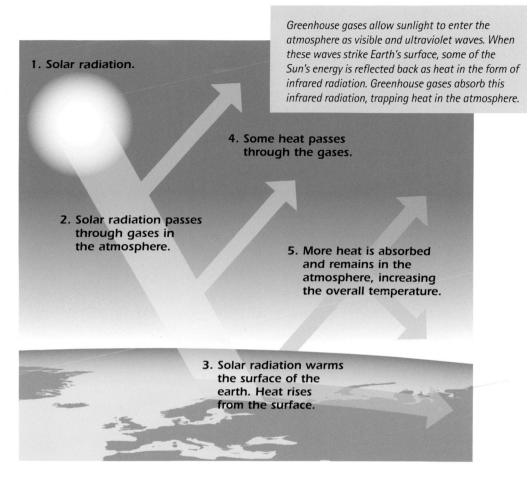

1. Solar radiation.

Greenhouse gases allow sunlight to enter the atmosphere as visible and ultraviolet waves. When these waves strike Earth's surface, some of the Sun's energy is reflected back as heat in the form of infrared radiation. Greenhouse gases absorb this infrared radiation, trapping heat in the atmosphere.

4. Some heat passes through the gases.

2. Solar radiation passes through gases in the atmosphere.

5. More heat is absorbed and remains in the atmosphere, increasing the overall temperature.

3. Solar radiation warms the surface of the earth. Heat rises from the surface.

Industrial pollution generated in the Great Lakes region is carried by northeasterly winds into Canada. There, acid rain has damaged or killed millions of trees and polluted some 14,000 lakes. Acid rain is declining in Europe and North America as a result of initiatives to reduce sulphur dioxide emissions. But elsewhere in the world, particularly in Asia, emissions are rising. In 2002, sulphur dioxide emissions in China from coal-burning power plants reached 7.2 million tons (a tenth of the world total). Large areas of China are now affected by acid rain, and in the Sichuan Basin region acid rain has destroyed 1,100 square miles (2,800 square kilometers) of forest, an area almost four times the size of New York City.

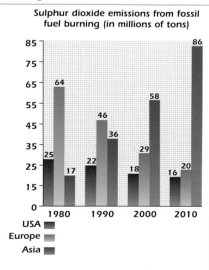

Sulphur dioxide emissions from fossil fuel burning (in millions of tons)

USA
Europe
Asia

	1980	1990	2000	2010
USA	25	22	18	16
Europe	64	46	29	20
Asia	17	36	58	86

Source: United Nations Environmental Program

Global warming

Earth is warming up. The ten hottest years on record have all occurred since 1990.

Most scientists believe that a major cause of this global warming is air pollution caused by human activity. Certain greenhouse gases occur naturally in the atmosphere and perform a crucial role in warming Earth's surface. However, additional emissions of greenhouse gases from human activity run into millions of tons over the past 100 years. For example, human activity pumps approximately 25 billion tons of carbon dioxide into the atmosphere every year. These additional greenhouse gases are believed to be the principal causes of global warming.

Gases that contribute to global warming.
Source: Atmospheric Research and Information Center

What is deforestation?

Deforestation also plays a major part in global warming. Often described as the "lungs of the planet," forests take in carbon dioxide from the air and generate much of the oxygen in Earth's atmosphere. Deforestation is the removal of forests, either cut down for their wood, to be used as a material or fuel, or cleared to create more land for farming or new settlements. In the past 40 years, 45 percent of the world's forests have disappeared. This has played a major part in reducing Earth's ability to convert carbon dioxide into oxygen.

Top emitters of carbon dioxide from fossil fuels 1900-1999

	Total emissions (millions of tons)	Percentage of world total
United States	85,230	30.3%
Russia	25,045	8.9%
Germany	20,551	7.3%
China	19,605	7.0%
United Kingdom	15,912	5.6%
Japan	10,317	3.7%
France	7,981	2.8%
Ukraine	6,592	2.3%
Canada	6,427	2.3%
Poland	5,729	2.0%
India	5,619	2.0%
Italy	4,617	1.6%
South Africa	3,475	1.2%
Australia	3,015	1.1%
Czech Republic	2,827	1.0%

Source: World Resources Institute

What effects will global warming bring?

Global warming is a complex process and no one is exactly certain what will occur in the future. A rise in global temperature of just 4 or 5°F (2 or 3 °C) could have a major impact on the planet. **Climate** change would lead to farmlands suffering, large areas of land becoming desert, and many species of plants and animals either migrating (moving) from the region or dying out. Many scientists believe that global warming could increase the speed at which the water cycle occurs. This would potentially create more violent weather phenomena, such as storms, hurricanes, floods, and droughts.

As global temperatures increase, sea levels will rise. The planet's ice caps will melt, the warmer water will expand and occupy more room than cooler water. Sea levels rose an estimated 8–12 inches (20–30 centimeters) in the 20th century, and many experts predict a further rise of 16–31 inches (40–80 centimeters) throughout the 21st century. This rise would put at risk some of the world's largest food-growing areas that lie near the coast or around river deltas. Much of the food grown in China, Egypt, Bangladesh, and Vietnam, for example, is on land less than 10 feet (3 meters) above sea level.

Tuvalu under threat

Just a three-foot rise in sea level would submerge most of the land of the island nations of the Maldives, Marshall Islands, and Tuvalu, among others. Tuvalu consists of nine small islands in the Pacific Ocean, near Fiji, which are all less than 15 feet (5 meters) above sea level. Rising sea levels are claiming valuable land and contaminating freshwater drinking wells with seawater. Tuvalu's 11,000 islanders face an uncertain future.

Air travel has boomed and today it contributes roughly 600 million tons of carbon dioxide into the atmosphere each year. This is nearly one-third of the entire output of the United States. There are also concerns that it will rise since the number of international air travelers is projected to double by 2018.

Water Pollution

Water is fundamental to life on Earth. It covers almost three quarters of the planet's surface, but most is seawater. Only 0.07 percent is available for use by people. This is the freshwater in lakes, rivers, and underground sources known as **aquifers**.

Water storage in the atmosphere

Condensation

Water storage in ice and snow

Precipitation

Snowmelt

Infiltration

Streamflow

Surface runoff

Evaporation

Ground water discharge

Freshwater storage

Ground water storage

Water storage in oceans

The water on the planet is constantly on the move, driven by heat energy from the Sun. It circulates from the land, water, and atmosphere in an endless sequence known as the water cycle.

Point source and non-point source pollution

Water pollution sources are often divided into two types. Point source is where pollutants reach water through a specific entry point, such as an oil tanker spillage or a drainpipe discharging sewage. Non-point source (NPS) pollution comes from different sources and can be harder to control. A common example of NPS pollution is runoff. This occurs when rain or melting snow washes over land, picks up pollutants along the way, and eventually carries them into lakes and rivers. Oil, grease, and salt from roads, animal and human waste, and chemicals from industry and agriculture can all be NPS pollutants.

Industrial pollution

Industry generates pollution in a variety of ways. Some of these, such as buried waste on land and certain forms of air pollution (such as acid rain) can be transformed into water pollution. Factories are often located near a river so that water can be used in their work. Sometimes they pump poisonous chemical waste into the water. Heat can also be a water pollutant. Power stations and other factories are often built near a river or sea to use large amounts of water as a coolant. In some situations, returning this water, now much warmer, to the natural water source can damage the **ecosystem.**

Dumping

Rivers, lakes, and seas have been used as dumping grounds for unwanted objects and substances for centuries. The problem became far more serious during the 20th century with the massive increase in waste and consumer goods and the rise of the chemical and nuclear power industries. Between 1946 and 1965, a site off the coast near San Francisco was used as a dumping ground for an estimated 47,000 barrels of radioactive waste. These 55-gallon barrels litter a large area on the ocean floor, and many experts fear the containers may have leaked and may have a long-term impact on marine life.

The world's most polluted water

Radioactive waste from nuclear power plants can also generate water pollution. Lake Karachai sits in western Siberia, Russia. Radioactive waste from the nearby Mayak nuclear power plant was pumped into the lake for almost twenty years. It is believed that the lake contains more **radioactivity** than was released by the entire Chernobyl nuclear accident, which is estimated to be 400 times the radioactive contamination released by the atomic bomb dropped on Hiroshima. Lake Karachai lies within the Chelyabinsk region, which has one of the highest cancer rates in Russia.

Agricultural water pollution

Fertilizers are used to help crops grow all over the world. Fertilizer use has increased to 160 million tons a year, ten times the amount used 50 years ago. More and more fertilizer chemicals, such as phosphates and nitrates, have found their way through soil and rock into underground water sources, or been washed by rain from the fields into nearby streams and rivers. Also, liquid animal manure (known as slurry) that is spread on farmland, and poisonous **herbicide** and **pesticide** chemicals used to kill weeds and insect pests, find their way into water sources. Some farm animals are carriers of bacteria that cause diseases such as E.coli, and cases exist where farm animals have contaminated water supplies.

An engineer inspects the pollution pouring from a pipeline into this lake.

Impacts on life

Water pollution can cause numerous problems. Both animals and humans can be poisoned by water containing radioactive pollutants, toxic industrial chemicals, and waste **heavy metals,** such as arsenic, mercury, and lead. Sewage and other pollutants in water can help transmit disease. Pollutants in water are sometimes absorbed by plants or consumed by creatures, causing these pollutants to enter the food chain. For example, cadmium, a heavy metal found in some fertilizers, can be absorbed by crops. If these crops are eaten in large enough amounts, they can cause diarrhea-based illnesses and liver and kidney damage.

Farmers who spray fertilizers on their crops need to wear protective masks.

Many forms of water pollution can cause oxygen to be used up or removed from water. For example, excess nitrogen can feed quick-growing **algae** that can block out sunlight and remove oxygen from the water. This can kill off life in lakes and areas of sea. More than 140 "dead zones"—where there is not enough oxygen for life to exist—are found in seas throughout the world, many off the eastern coast of the United States and in the seas in and around Europe.

The Gulf of Mexico dead zone

The Mississippi River system is America's largest and drains 41 percent of the mainland United States. Its waters carry up to 1.8 million tons of nitrogen into the Gulf of Mexico every year. Half of this comes from fertilizers used on farmland which has run off into streams and rivers that feed the Mississippi. The remainder comes from animal waste and industrial and sewage treatment waste water pumped into the Mississippi. This nitrogen has helped generate a gigantic dead zone in the Gulf of Mexico where little marine life exists. The dead zone is roughly 13,000 mi^2 (21,000km^2) in size, larger than the state of Maryland.

Oil and water

Oil can spill and spread over a large area of water, poisoning and killing plants and animals. According to the Oil Spill Intelligence Report, since 1960 there have been 49 spills of 37 tons of oil or more in the English Channel and 267 spills in the Gulf of Mexico. In August 2003, the *Tasmin Spirit* oil tanker spilled an estimated 16,500 tons along the coast of Pakistan. The oil devastated fishing grounds and put 90,000 Pakistani fishers out of work.

Although spills from damaged oil tankers like the *Amoco Cadiz* and the *Exxon Valdez* make the headlines, they only make up a fraction of the oil that pollutes water. Air pollution, mainly from cars and industry, puts hundreds of tons of pollutants from oil products into the oceans each year as rain washes these products out of the air and into oceans. The cleaning out of ship engines and tanker containers contributes to the oil pollution of oceans. Millions more gallons of used oil from motor vehicles and machinery find their way into waterways and oceans. More than half of all Americans, for example, change their own oil, but only about one-third of this used oil is collected and recycled.

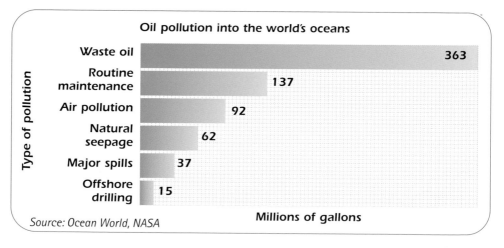

Oil pollution into the world's oceans

Type of pollution	Millions of gallons
Waste oil	363
Routine maintenance	137
Air pollution	92
Natural seepage	62
Major spills	37
Offshore drilling	15

Source: Ocean World, NASA

Access to water

We take clean water for granted, but millions of people are affected by dry climates and droughts, which mean a lack of water in their region. Many millions more live near freshwater sources, but ones which have been seriously polluted and are not safe to drink, wash, or cook with. The **United Nations (UN)** estimates that more than 1.1 billion people lack access to a regular, clean, and safe water supply. The vast majority of these people live in the world's poorest nations.

Water, poverty, and disease

- The average American uses 183 gallons (692 liters) of water per day.
- The average person in the developing world uses 2.6 gallons (10 liters) per day.
- 40 billion hours are spent every year carrying water by people (mainly women) in Africa.
- Every 8 seconds, a child dies from a water-related disease.
- 50 percent of people in developing countries suffer from a water-related disease.

Source: United Nations

This water standpipe, provided by the charity WaterAid, offers clean water to people who previously had to rely on polluted river sources. In 2002-2003, WaterAid helped more than 640,000 people gain access to clean water supplies.

The problem of sewage

Vast amounts of sewage containing waste water from households and human waste is pumped into rivers, lakes, and seas. In wealthier, more developed countries, much of this is treated to remove some of the key pollutants. But half the world's population live in areas without adequate sewage systems and where sewage tends to be flushed straight back into streams and rivers without being treated. For example, Bangkok, the capital city of Thailand, discharges an estimated 12,000 tons of raw sewage and other waste into its rivers and canals every day.

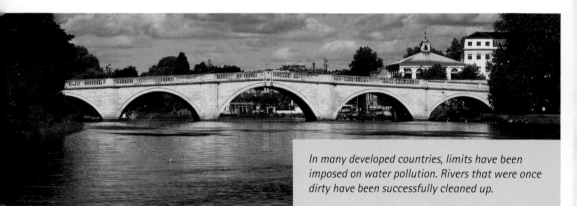

In many developed countries, limits have been imposed on water pollution. Rivers that were once dirty have been successfully cleaned up.

Many deadly diseases are carried or caused by this polluted water, either through eating food contaminated with this water, or by organisms such as bacteria that breed in the water. Water-related diseases, such as cholera, diarrhea, and trachoma (which causes blindness or major health problems in six million people) is responsible for the deaths of more than 5.2 million people every year.

Access to safe water and life expectancy in selected countries, 2002

Country	Percentage of population without access to clean water	Life expectancy at birth (in years)
Afghanistan	87	43
Ethiopia	76	42
Chad	73	48
Sierra Leone	72	39
Angola	62	47
Papua New Guinea	58	42
Uganda	50	42
Vietnam	44	69
China	25	70
United States	0	77
United Kingdom	0	77

Source: World Bank, 2002

Cleaning up the world's water

Although it can take large amounts of money and a long time, water pollution can be reduced and its effects reversed. Large remediation (clean-up) operations can help improve water quality, but new laws, agreements, and systems are essential to stop further pollution from occurring.

There have been successes. Phosphate levels in two of the Great Lakes, Lake Ontario and Lake Erie, have dropped by more than 75 percent since the 1970s. In the United Kingdom, the River Thames was so polluted that in 1949 water samples from the river contained no oxygen. Yet, following major clean-up initiatives and stricter laws, the water quality has improved so much that in 2000, more than 90 species of fish were found in its waters. But much more needs to be done to enable far more of the world's water to be clean and safe for all life.

Low-cost initiatives to help treat sewage effectively and to reduce water pollution are being developed: using beds of reeds, shown here, can absorb some of the pollutants in sewage and water naturally.

Land Pollution

Land pollution is the degrading of Earth's land. It can occur on different scales and cause harm in many ways. Litter, such as old wire or fishing line, can strangle birds and land animals. Large-scale burying or dumping of toxic chemicals on land can pollute and harm life over a large area.

Pollution on land is often then transferred into water. Water that seeps through a landfill or toxic waste dump can carry some of the harmful pollutants from the land into water sources.

Garbage dumps

Most wealthier, developed countries generate millions of tons of solid waste or garbage. In the United States, for example, an estimated 1,600 pounds (720 kilograms) of waste is generated per year for every person who lives there. Every family in the United Kingdom generates approximately a ton of household garbage per year.

This waste is disposed of in a number of ways, such as being burned in **incinerators**. Roughly half of all of the household waste in the United States and more than 80 percent of waste in the United Kingdom is buried in dumps in the ground, called landfill sites. When full, most landfill sites in wealthier countries are landscaped and all looks well on the surface.

But environmentalists are concerned about what may be going on underneath. As the buried garbage **decomposes**, it can form poisonous substances. Rainwater seeps through a landfill site and can produce a poisonous liquid called leachate. The leachate may then enter underground water supplies, or even streams and rivers.

The decomposing garbage can also generate large amounts of methane gas which, if not managed, can cause explosions. **Sanitary** landfill sites have been developed that provide a solid plastic or concrete barrier between the waste materials and the soil, but some environmentalists still fear that these barriers could be damaged and release pollutants into the soil and **groundwater**.

Love Canal

Throughout the 20th century, Love Canal in New York was an abandoned canal that was used as a dumping ground for an estimated 25,000 tons of poisonous chemicals from industry. The canal was filled in with soil and roughly 100 houses and a school were built on the land. By the late 1970s, several hazardous chemicals had leaked through their metal containers or had risen to the surface. Investigations confirmed that poisonous substances were in the soil and that the area had high rates of birth defects, cancer, and other illnesses. Families were evacuated in 1978 and the site declared a national emergency. In the mid-1990s, the chemical company that owned the land agreed to pay national and state governments a total of $227 million in compensation.

Pesticide pollution

As the world's population has boomed, the demand on farmland to produce more food has greatly increased. Most farmers have started using chemical pesticides to kill insects that can harm or reduce the yield of a crop. Many of these pesticide chemicals can build to levels that harm the soil's ability to support crops and other life. They can also pollute water supplies. In the early 1990s, the United Nations estimated that some five million people a year suffer from serious pesticide poisoning. Persistent Organic Pollutants (POPs) are chemical substances that stay in the environment over a long period of time. There is great concern about POPs as they enter the food chain and build up in the fatty tissues of animals. Many POPs are pesticides.

Tackling land pollution

We can fight land pollution in a number of ways. Some chemical pesticides and herbicides have been outlawed in many countries, although the polluting effects from their use in the past will take many years to disappear. Farming using natural, non-chemical forms of pest and weed control is an important way to lower chemical levels in the soil. Major community **recycling** plans can also help reduce waste levels and save energy and resources.

Consumer demand for produce grown without pesticides has led to the expansion of organic farms in the developing world. Organic tea (left) is now widely available.

Individuals can make a difference in a number of ways. They can greatly reduce the amount of waste they generate by following the "three Rs":

- Reducing consumption (by buying longer-lasting items and items with less or no packaging)
- Reusing old items (by repairing damaged items and donating old items)
- Recycling waste like paper, plastic bottles, glass, and aluminum soda cans.

Biodegradable

Many materials are biodegradable. This means they can rot and break down relatively quickly and safely by natural means and be absorbed into the environment. Cotton rags, for example, can take between one and five months to break down. Other materials do not break down as quickly. Plastic bags can take 10-20 years, tin cans 50-100 years, and glass bottles a million years.

U.S. household waste (pounds per person a year)

	1960	1980	2003
Total waste	949	1,336	1,587
Waste recycled	61	121	498

Source: United States Environmental Protection Agency (EPA)

Most plastics take a long time to break down and are a serious threat to wildlife. Every year, up to two million seabirds die as a result of eating, or get tangled up in, garbage.

The Debate over Solutions

Pollution causes harm all over the world. What is being done to tackle it? Many different initiatives are being introduced or worked on throughout the world. Some are based on technological breakthroughs, others as a result of national laws or international agreements between countries. Many more are the work of communities of ordinary people trying to fight pollution in their local area.

Cleaner energy sources

Most of the world's electricity is generated by burning fossil fuels that release harmful pollutants into the atmosphere. Things can be improved, though. Devices called scrubbers remove as much as 95 percent of sulphur dioxide and nitrogen dioxide emissions from electricity-generating power plants. The United States and Canada, for example, reduced their sulphur dioxide emissions by 28 percent between 1980 and 1995. By 2010 their goal is to cut emissions from 1980 levels in half.

Some countries have switched from power stations that burn coal to less polluting stations that burn **natural gas**. However, even natural gas power stations send large amounts of pollutants into the air.

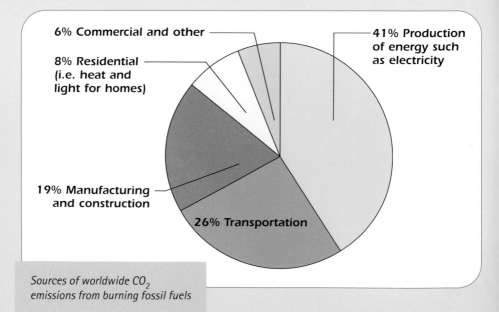

6% Commercial and other

8% Residential (i.e. heat and light for homes)

41% Production of energy such as electricity

19% Manufacturing and construction

26% Transportation

Sources of worldwide CO_2 emissions from burning fossil fuels

ALTERNATIVE ENERGY

Alternative energy sources exist that are not only renewable, but also generate little or no pollution. Except for some noise pollution and the pollution generated in building them, wind turbines emit no dangerous substances as their blades turn to produce electricity. The same is true for solar panels and thermal water heaters, both of which use energy from the Sun. Critics of renewable energies maintain that they cannot supply the vast amounts of energy demanded by growing populations. But those in favor point out that they can make a major contribution to providing energy while greatly reducing pollution.

NUCLEAR POWER

Nuclear power is one of the least polluting of all major energy sources. It sends no emissions into the atmosphere and uses only small amounts of fuel to generate large amounts of electricity. Some countries with great increases in energy demand, such as India, are building new nuclear power stations. But a major accident at a nuclear power plant could bring catastrophic damage, and this has raised public fears. Public protests have stopped the development of nuclear power and closed down power stations in many countries.

This bus, powered by a hydrogen fuel cell, is one of a new generation of cleaner vehicles.

Cleaner travel and transportation

The fossil fuels burned by cars, trucks, and planes are a major source of air pollution, while discarded motor vehicles, fuels, and products such as car batteries pollute water and land. Yet, just like the demand for electricity, the number of motor vehicles in the world is expected to rise dramatically. In India's capital city, New Delhi, transportation accounts for 65 percent of all air pollution. In the last 25 years, the population has increased three times, but motor vehicle numbers have increased nearly 13 times.

Some countries have passed stricter laws on emissions from cars. They encourage carpooling and strive to improve public transportation, which is more energy efficient and generates less pollution per passenger per trip. Technology has provided improvements such as lead-free gasoline and cars that are more fuel-efficient. The brightest prospect is for vehicles powered by non-fossil fuels, such as hydrogen, that generates zero air pollution.

Fuel efficiency of different types of vehicles can be measured in terms of how far a gallon of fuel can carry a passenger.

One gallon of fuel carries a passenger:
- 9 miles (14 kilometers) in a large car
- 12 miles (19 kilometers) in a small car
- 67 miles (108 kilometers) in a 40-seater bus

A hazy smog caused by atmospheric pollution is clearly visible over the city of Cairo in Egypt.

International laws and agreements

While some pollution problems are found inside national borders, the most severe pollution issues the world faces are international. Agreements between nations to reduce pollution have had some success. For example, MARPOL is a United Nations treaty that became effective in 1983. It helped to reduce oil pollution at sea by almost 60 percent during the 1980s and early 1990s. The **Montreal Protocol**, established in 1987, was designed to reduce the emissions of CFCs that threatened the ozone layer. World CFC production fell by 91 percent between 1986 and 2002. The ozone layer is still being depleted as a result of CFCs in the past, but scientists estimate that the depletion has already slowed down by more than half.

The Kyoto Protocol

To some critics, international agreements are a good idea but mean nothing unless they are enforced fully and by all countries. The Kyoto Protocol of 1997 gave every industrial country a target to control and reduce its greenhouse gas emissions by 5.2 percent by 2012. A number of nations are on target to reach their goal, but the agreement has had many problems. Some critics argue that a 5 percent cut is simply not enough to make a difference, and not all nations who initially signed the agreement are enforcing their reductions. The United States, responsible for a quarter of the total world CO_2 emissions, has not agreed to the protocol due to various reasons, including the strain some believe it would put on the U.S. economy.

UNITED TO FIGHT CLIMATE CHANGE
KYOTO PROTOCOL 16-2-2005

In 2005, the Kyoto Protocol, which had been agreed upon in 1997, came into force. At the conference held to commemorate this achievement, there was still much discussion about what countries could be doing to reduce emissions further.

Short term vs. long term

Scientists believe that many of the effects of pollution on the environment can be stopped or reversed. But they also believe that it will take a large effort. Since many pollutants have a long life—CFCs, for example, can last more than 100 years in the atmosphere—it will also take a long time.

Most people think only about the present and the next couple of years ahead. Many governments are elected to power for short periods of four or five years. While the majority of people believe a less polluted, cleaner environment is a good thing, they are reluctant to reduce their high standard of living or to pay higher taxes or prices for goods and energy produced. Industries also put pressure on governments, arguing that slashing pollution would greatly increase costs and force them to put people out of work and raise prices.

Cleaning up Lake Taihu

A five-year program is underway to clean up the third largest freshwater lake in China, Lake Taihu. The lake, a major source of drinking water for some 40 million people, has been heavily polluted by untreated sewage, pesticides, fertilizers, and industrial waste. There are 243 different projects, including 81 sewage disposal plants, being built at a cost of $2.6 billion. This figure is likely to increase since pollution levels in the lake are still rising. A major part of the problem is that local industries ignore the new laws and continue to pump pollution into the lake.

Costs of pollution

Some people want to see strict pollution guidelines imposed on every nation, but many poorer, developing nations argue that this is unfair. The poorest nations consume a fraction of the goods, services, and energy of the wealthiest nations. Many poorer countries are developing their industries to try to provide their people with a higher standard of living and this, in turn, is generating increasing levels of pollution. Do people in these nations have the right to electricity just like the majority of the world's population, even if that were to create more pollution?

Clearing up and reducing future pollution costs large sums of money. Many poorer countries, struggling to provide the most basic of services to their people, argue that they simply cannot afford to use the cleanest energy and manufacturing techniques. Many of these nations also point out that it is the wealthier countries that have generated most of the world's pollution. Just 15 countries, including the United States, the United Kingdom, Germany, Japan, and France, generate 79 percent of all CO_2 emissions. Many less developed nations question why they should be forced to agree to decisions made by more developed countries that have been both the biggest polluters in the past, and remain so today.

Improving the terrible living conditions endured by many of their people may be more of a priority for governments in developing countries than enforcing international decisions on pollution control.

A Clean Future?

Many of the things people do that cause pollution are likely to increase in the near future. The world's population is rising and may top eight billion by 2030. Two thirds of the world's people are expected to live in cities by that time. More countries are seeking to develop their industries. Motor vehicle numbers are increasing and, if they increase at the present rate, will reach more than one billion by 2025. Many predictions for the future are gloomy. Global warming is expected to have a major impact on the planet later in the 21st century. The World Health Organization estimates that by 2025 as many as eight million people per year could die due to pollution-related health problems unless massive attempts are made to stop the rising tide of air, water, and land pollution.

Many environmental groups organize activities that young people can get involved in. Here, volunteers collect garbage from a beach.

Advances in energy-efficient technology and the growing use of non-polluting **renewable energy** sources and vehicle fuels would help. Stricter international agreements and tough laws in individual countries will probably be necessary. But these will only work if they are backed by large amounts of money to fund alternative ways of producing goods and services. Finally, individuals must make small but crucial changes in the way that they live. As shown by the large drop in sulphur dioxide emissions in some countries, and the global lowering of CFCs, there have already been notable breakthroughs and successes. But much, much more must be done if the world population is going to enjoy as clean and unpolluted a planet as their ancestors did in the past.

Ten things you can do to help reduce pollution

- Walk or bicycle short journeys instead of taking a car. Encourage your family, neighbors, and friends to do the same.
- Make your home use less energy by turning off lights, installing energy efficient compact fluorescent light bulbs, and by setting heating and air conditioning levels to use less energy.
- Boil only the amount of water you need. Every cup boiled uses electricity that equals approximately 25 cups of released carbon dioxide.
- Many electrical items still consume electricity when plugged in. Unplug all electrical items when not in use.
- Use phosphate-free detergents and cleaning products.
- Use rechargeable batteries rather than disposable ones.
- Start a local or community program to plant trees in your neighborhood.
- Recycle paper, glass, aluminum, and other materials.
- Reuse as many objects and materials, such as plastic bags, as possible. This saves both energy and waste, both of which can cause pollution.
- Investigate where pollution prevention and clean-up programs exist in your area and join in.

Statistical Information

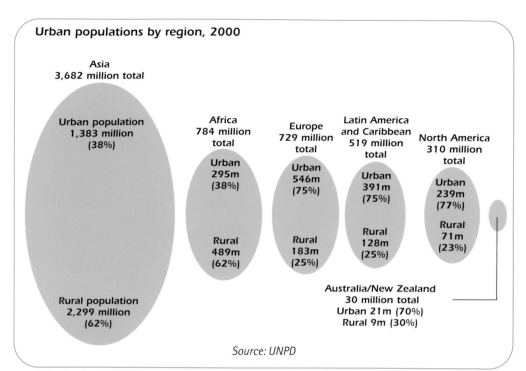

Urban populations by region, 2000

Asia
3,682 million total

Urban population
1,383 million
(38%)

Rural population
2,299 million
(62%)

Africa
784 million
total

Urban
295m
(38%)

Rural
489m
(62%)

Europe
729 million
total

Urban
546m
(75%)

Rural
183m
(25%)

Latin America
and Caribbean
519 million
total

Urban
391m
(75%)

Rural
128m
(25%)

North America
310 million
total

Urban
239m
(77%)

Rural
71m
(23%)

Australia/New Zealand
30 million total
Urban 21m (70%)
Rural 9m (30%)

Source: UNPD

Countries with greatest increase in motor vehicles 1980–1998

South Korea	1,514%
Thailand	692%
Nigeria	550%
China	300%
Pakistan	300%
Uganda	300%
Turkey	252%
India	250%
Poland	217%
Indonesia	175%

Source: World Bank

Top ten nitrogen oxide polluting countries

	Pounds of nitrogen oxide per person
Australia	260
Iceland	234
United States	176
Canada	150
Finland	112
Norway	112
Denmark	104
New Zealand	103
Czech Republic	90
Luxembourg	88

Source: Organization for Economic Cooperation and Development

Air pollution in selected world cities

City	Population (millions)	Suspended particles levels (mg/m³)	Sulphur dioxide levels (mg/m³)	Nitrogen dioxide levels (mg/m³)
		90*	50*	50*
Amsterdam	1.1	40	10	58
Athens	3.1	178	34	64
Beijing	11.3	377	90	122
Berlin	3.3	50	18	26
Brussels	1.1	78	20	48
Bombay	15.1	240	33	39
Cairo	9.9	–	69	–
Copenhagen	1.3	61	7	54
Dublin	0.9	–	20	–
Havana	2.2	–	1	5
Kuala Lumpur	1.2	85	24	–
London	7.6	–	25	77
Los Angeles	12.4	–	9	74
Mexico City	16.6	279	74	130
Milan	4.3	77	31	248
Montreal	3.3	34	10	42
Moscow	9.3	100	109	–
New York	16.3	–	26	79
Singapore	2.8	–	20	30
Sydney	3.6	54	28	–
Tokyo	27.0	49	18	68

Source: World Bank
* World Health Organization recommended maximum levels

Glossary

acid rain rain, snow, and fog
    containing poisonous or harmful
    acidic chemicals, created by
    burning fossil fuels
algae primitive plants, including
    seaweeds and pond scum
altitude height, usually above sea
    level, of a particular point
aquifer underground water supply,
    often tapped for domestic use
atmosphere collection of gases
    that surround Earth
atom smallest unit of matter
    that can take part in a
    chemical reaction

chlorofluorocarbons (CFCs)
    series of manmade chemicals
    used in refrigerators, aerosols,
    and solvents
cholera infectious disease of the
    small intestine that is carried
    by bacteria
climate general weather conditions
    of a region or the entire Earth
    over a long period of time

decompose become rotten

ecosystem collection of all living
    things and their non-living
    surroundings in a defined area
emission harmful gas released into
    the air by industry, fires, and
    motor vehicles

enhanced greenhouse effect
    build-up of carbon dioxide,
    methane, and other gases in the
    atmosphere, trapping the Sun's
    heat and affecting the climate
environment physical surroundings
epidemic rapid spread of disease
erode to wear away

fertilizer substance that enriches
    soil and enables it to support
    more plant growth
food chain links between different
    animals that feed on plants and
    other animals
fossil fuel material that has
    been formed from decayed
    living things, and can be burned
    to generate energy

global warming warming of
    Earth's surface due to changes in
    the gases within Earth's
    atmosphere
greenhouse gas gas in the
    atmosphere that traps heat from
    the Sun and warms Earth
groundwater water beneath
    Earth's surface that supplies the
    water tapped by wells, or that
    flows from springs

heavy metals metallic elements,
    such as cadmium, lead, and
    mercury, that can be poisonous
herbicide substance used as a
    weed killer when growing crops

incinerator device used to burn solid waste

industrialization process in which more and more emphasis is placed upon industry and manufacturing in a country's economy

ingest take a substance into the body, usually by eating or drinking

insecticide substance used to kill insects

methane natural gas

Montreal Protocol international agreement that defined targets and timetables for phasing out the use of CFCs

natural gas mixture of methane and other gases found underground or below the seabed, which can be used as a fuel

ozone layer thin layer of the atmosphere consisting of ozone gas. It absorbs most of the harmful ultraviolet rays from the Sun.

pesticide poisonous substance that kills animal or insect pests

PM10 microscopic particles in the atmosphere such as dust, dirt, smoke, and soot

radioactivity harmful rays and particles given off by certain substances as their atoms split apart

recycling recovering waste material to make new products. Can also mean to re-use discarded products.

renewable energy energy from a source that can be restored and maintained, such as wind and solar energy

resources natural things found on Earth, such as metals, trees, coal, or water, that can be used in production

respiration chemical process in which food is broken down to release energy

sanitary free from dirt or bacteria that can cause disease

sewage waste, usually including waste water and human sewage

smog haze caused by smoke or atmospheric pollution

toxic harmful or poisonous substance

ultraviolet invisible form of light from the Sun that causes sunburn and can cause blindness and cancer

United Nations (UN) international organization, founded in 1945 to promote peace, security, and economic development

urban to do with the city or town

World Health Organization (WHO) international body concerned with the health and wellbeing of the planet's population

Further Reading

Baines, John. *Keeping The Air Clean*. Chicago: Raintree, 1998.
Written by an award-winning environmentalist, this book looks in detail at the technical issues surrounding the many causes and forms of air pollution and the potential solutions.

Chapman, Matthew and Bowden, Rob. *21st Century Debates: Air Pollution*. Chicago: Raintree, 2002.
This book gives a detailed look at the issue of air pollution, its causes, and its impacts, with a number of case studies from around the world.

Collinson, Alan. *Pollution*. London: Evans Brothers, 1997.
Part of a series studying natural and manmade disasters, this book traces the history of human impact on Earth and the pollution people have generated from ancient times until the end of the 20th century.

Cooper, Adrian, Bowden, Rob and Bingley, Richard. *Just The Facts: Global Pollution*. Chicago: Heinemann, 2002.
This is a clear, simple guide to world pollution, filled with statistics.

Contact Addresses

Australian Conservation
Foundation (ACF)
Floor 1
60 Leicester Street
Carlton
Victoria 3053
Australia
Tel: 03 9345 1111

Canadian Centre for Pollution
Prevention (C2P2)
100 Charlotte Street
Sarnia
Ontario
N7T 4R2
Canada
Tel: (1 800) 667 9790

Earth Policy Institute
1350 Connecticut Avenue, NW
Suite 403
Washington DC 20036
Tel: (202) 496-9290

Friends of the Earth
26-28 Underwood Street
London
N1 7JQ
UK
Tel: 020 7490 1555

National Society for Clean Air and
Environmental Protection – NSCA
44 Grand Parade
Brighton
BN2 2QA
UK
Tel: 01273 878770

Worldwatch Institute
1776 Massachusetts Avenue, NW
Washington, DC 20036
Tel (202) 452-1999

Websites

Center for Renewable Energy and Sustainable Technology
http://www.crest.org/
This website includes news and information on energy application in the
United States.

Greenpeace
http://www.greenpeace.org
The international organization which promotes environmental awareness
and understanding has comprehensive news and report sections on
climate change.

National Oceanic and Atmospheric Administration
http://response.restoration.noaa.gov/kids/kids.html
A dedicated younger reader's section of this website has a detailed
breakdown of the issue of oil pollution of water and land, and looks at
attempts at prevention and clean–up operations.

World Health Organization
http://www.who.int/topics/en/
A collection of topics that concern the World Health Organization (WHO),
including indoor air pollution, water quality, and waste management are
discussed on this site.

Index